Perfection Learning®

Robots

Stanley Ling

Contents

Introduction 3
What Robots Can Do 4
Robots All Around Us 8
    Shear Magic 8
    Meldog 8
    Robosaurus 9
Programming a Robot .10
Being a Robot 11
    The Task: To Move Objects
        from a Bowl to a Plate 11
    Discussing the Rules 12
    Moving the Objects 13
Making a Robot 14
    Making the Eyes 18
Glossary 23
Index 24

This robot can move its arms and legs.

Introduction

A robot is a machine that can move and do work **automatically** in place of a human. Robots are often used when a job is very dangerous, dirty, or boring.

A car wash is a type of robot. Think of a job you have to do that you would like a robot to do for you.

We sometimes use the word *robot* to mean a machine that looks like a person. These robots are usually in films, like *Star Wars*.

What Robots Can Do

Robots can only do what they are programmed to do. Many robots have parts made like arms and hands that allow them to move like humans. Robots can help humans in many different situations.

Robots have been sent into space to do jobs where humans could not work.

Some robots are used in space.

Robots are able to do jobs that humans find boring.

Robots are used to make cars. Imagine how you would feel painting the same part of a car 1000 times every day. A robot does not have feelings or a nose to get stuffed with paint spray!

Some robots do jobs that could be very dangerous for people to do. They can take bombs apart. These robots have to be made from very strong metal, in case the bombs blow up.

Mining underground can be a very unhealthy, dangerous job for humans. So robots are used to dig tunnels and check for harmful gas.

This robot is making a bomb safe.

Very small tools are used in some operations.

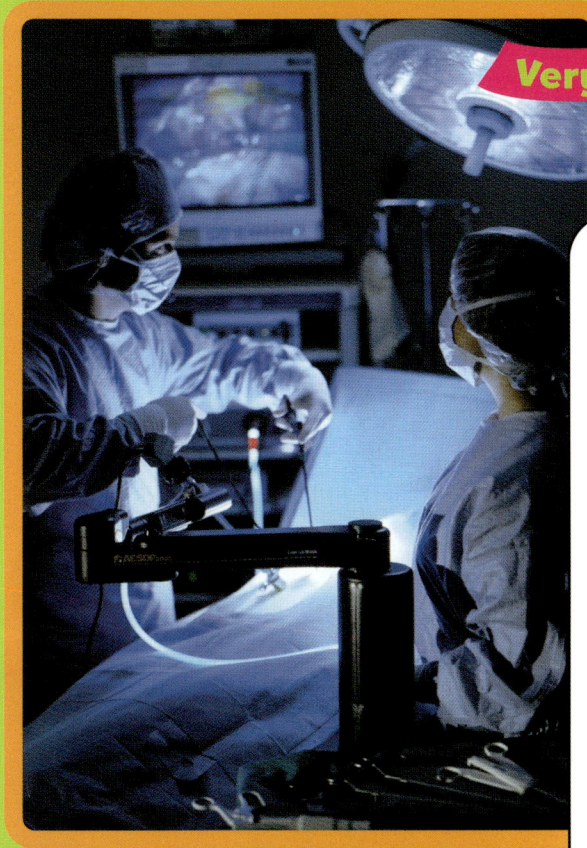

Robots can be used in deep water where it is very cold. They are not harmed by the cold, as a human would be. And because robots do not need to breathe, they can go on working until the job is finished!

Robots are used in medicine. They help in operations where tiny tools are needed. The robots can easily make small, precise movements.

Robots All Around Us

Shear Magic

The Shear Magic robot is used on sheep farms. **Shearing** is usually done by humans. It is a difficult job because the sheep wriggle about. Shear Magic has a cradle to hold the sheep safely while the robot arms clip the wool.

Meldog

This robot can do the job of a guide dog. It can help people who are blind or cannot see properly. Meldog uses sensors to detect things that are in the way.

A robot dog

Robosaurus in action

Robosaurus

This very big robot is used to entertain people. It is taller than a giraffe and six times heavier than an elephant.

Robosaurus is driven by a person strapped into the body of the robot. When the driver moves an arm, Robosaurus's arm moves the same way. The driver uses foot pedals to make Robosaurus walk backward and forward.

Robosaurus is programmed to use a flamethrower and crush cars, just like a monster in a film.

Programming a Robot

Robots need to be told what to do. They are not **intelligent**. They have computer **programs** to control their movements.

A person decides on the instructions and rules that will control the robot.

If you wanted a robot to brush your dog, you might start by telling it to move the brush up and down. But you might also have to tell it not to go too fast or too hard. All the instructions are written into the computer program.

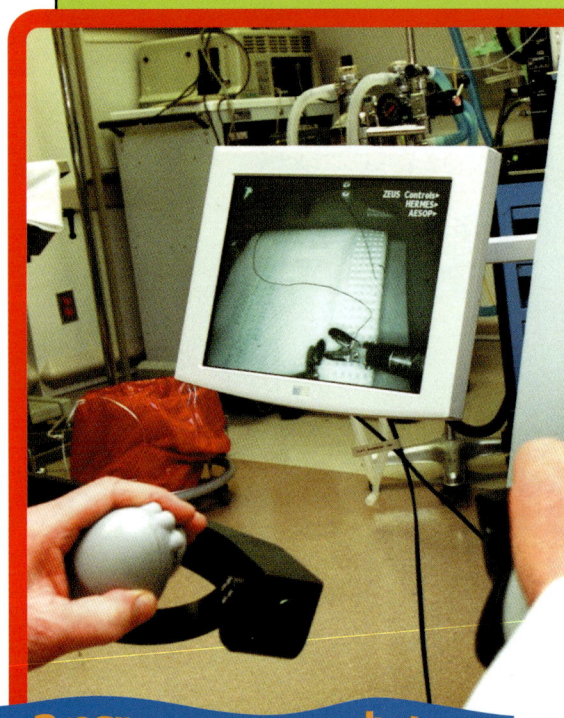

Programming a robot

Being a Robot

The Task: To Move Objects from a Bowl to a Plate

You will need:
- a partner
- a bowl
- small objects to put in the bowl
- a plate
- a chair
- a table
- a blindfold
- pen/pencil
- paper

What to do: Setting up

1. Put the plate on the table.
2. Put the objects into the bowl.
3. Put the chair beside the table.
4. Decide who will be the robot and who will be the programmer.

Discussing the Rules

1. Can the robot walk around?
2. Can anyone tell it what to do?
3. How fast can it move?
4. Can it use both arms?
5. Where should it stand?
6. Write your rules down.
7. Predict what movements your robot will need to complete the task.
8. Write down your instructions.

Robots on a car assembly line

Moving the Objects

1. Blindfold the robot person.
2. Check that the area is safe for your experiment.
3. Program your robot by reading your rules and instructions aloud.
4. Watch the robot move the objects.
5. Did the robot manage to move all the objects onto the plate?
6. Did the instructions work well?
7. What changes would you make to your program?

Making a Robot

Now that you have read and thought about robots, perhaps you would like to make a model robot of your own.

You will need:

- 4 cardboard tubes
- 1 big rectangular cardboard box
- 1 medium square cardboard box
- 2 small square cardboard boxes
- tape
- paints and paintbrush

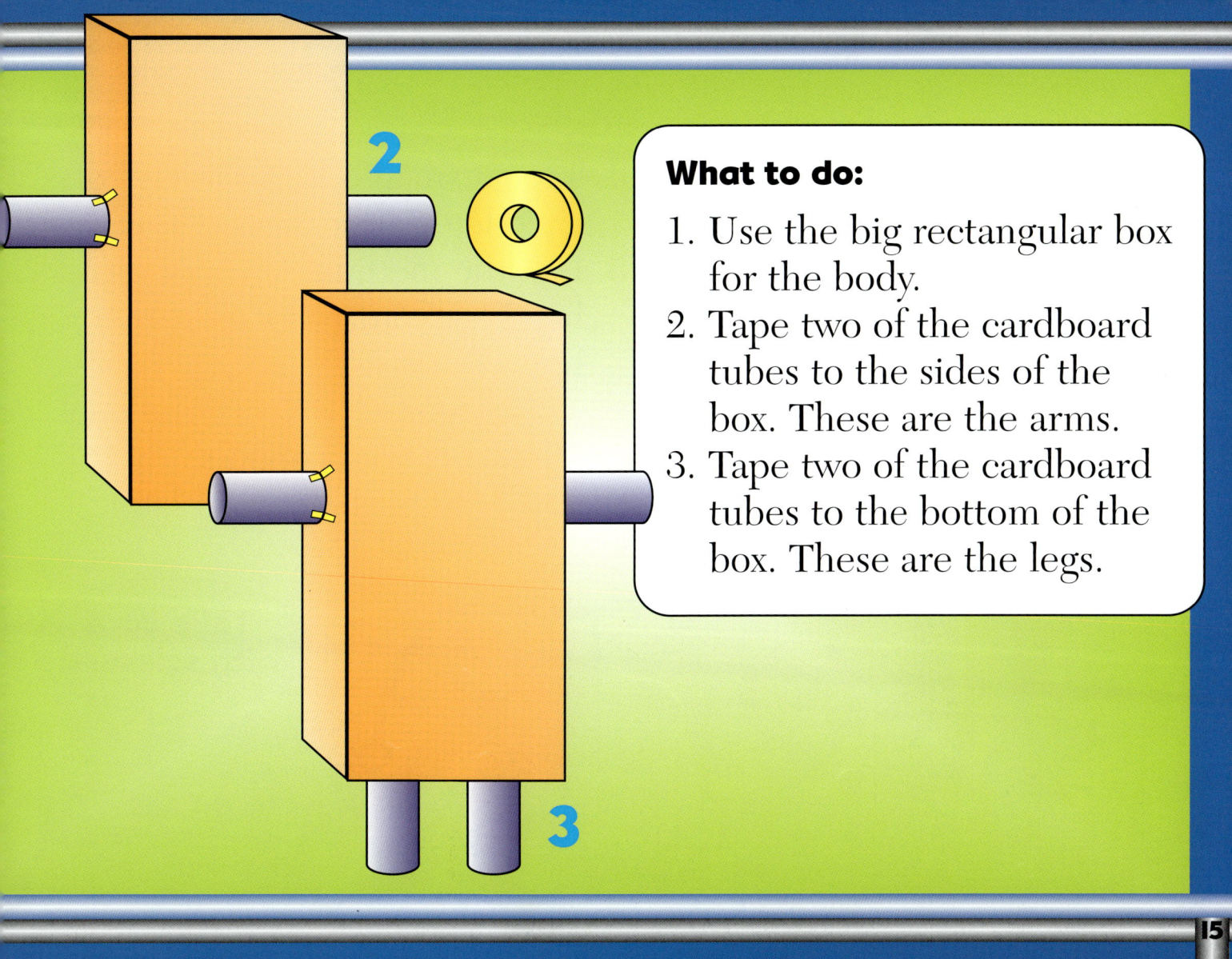

What to do:

1. Use the big rectangular box for the body.
2. Tape two of the cardboard tubes to the sides of the box. These are the arms.
3. Tape two of the cardboard tubes to the bottom of the box. These are the legs.

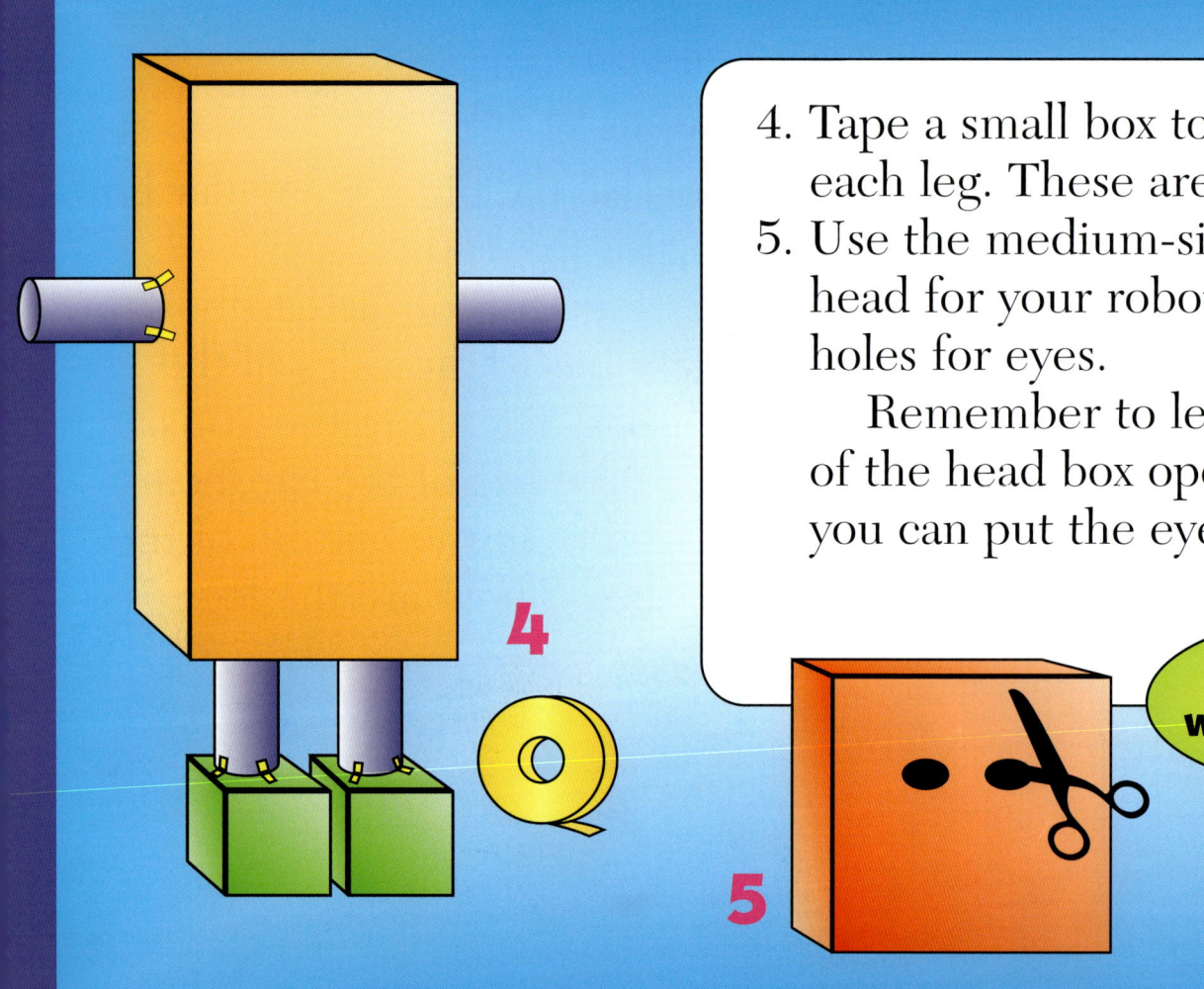

4. Tape a small box to the end of each leg. These are the feet.
5. Use the medium-size box as a head for your robot. Cut two holes for eyes.

   Remember to leave the back of the head box open so that you can put the eyes in later.

Take care with scissors!

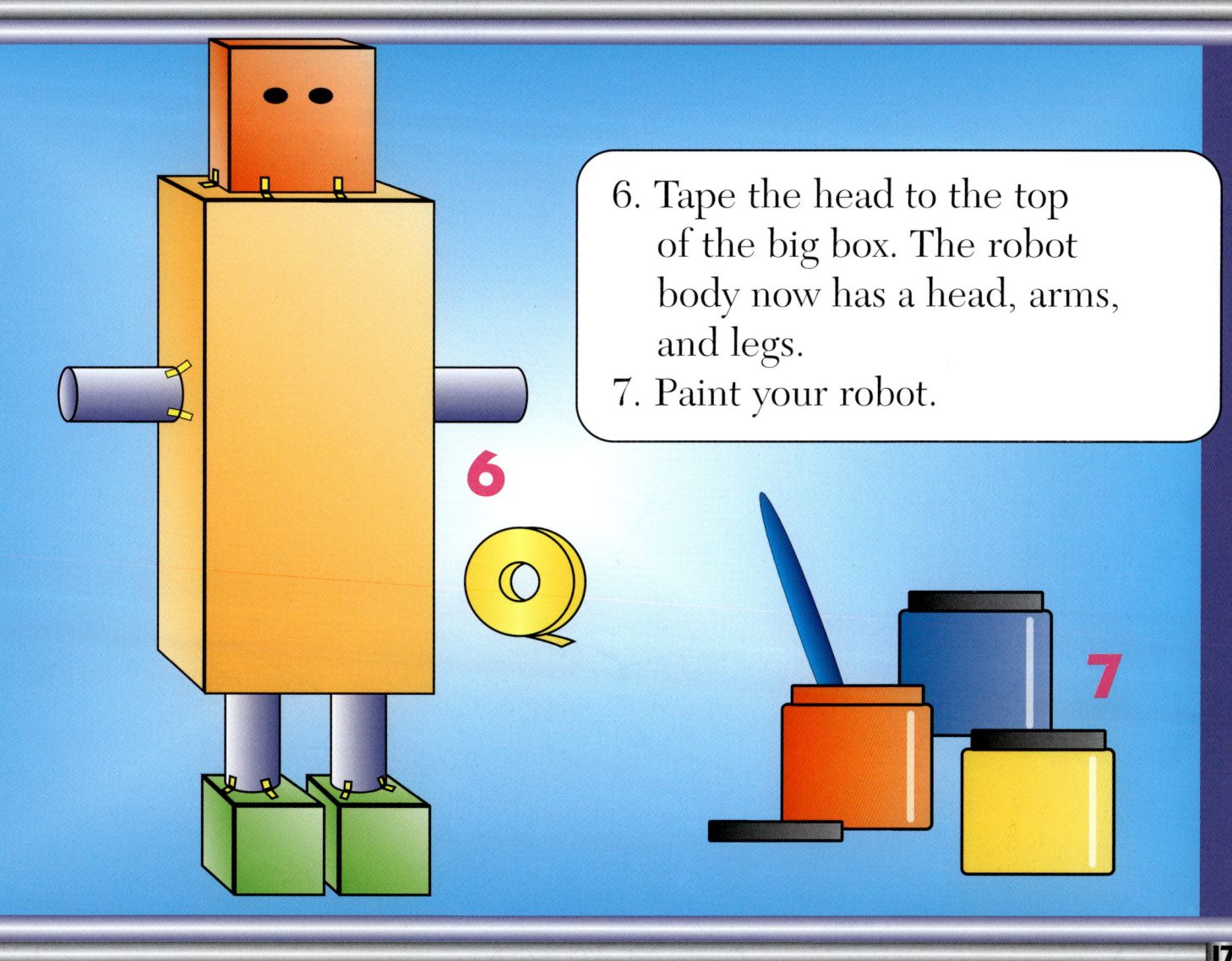

6. Tape the head to the top of the big box. The robot body now has a head, arms, and legs.
7. Paint your robot.

Making the Eyes

You will need:

- 2 small lightbulb holders
- 2 small lightbulbs
- 4 wires
- 1 battery
- 1 battery holder
- 1 paper clip

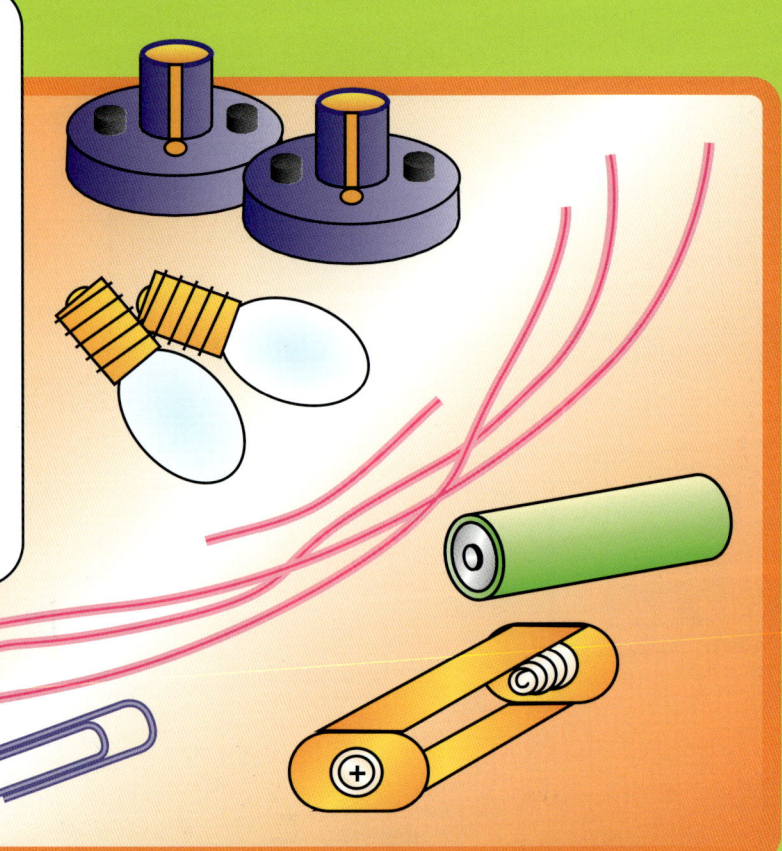

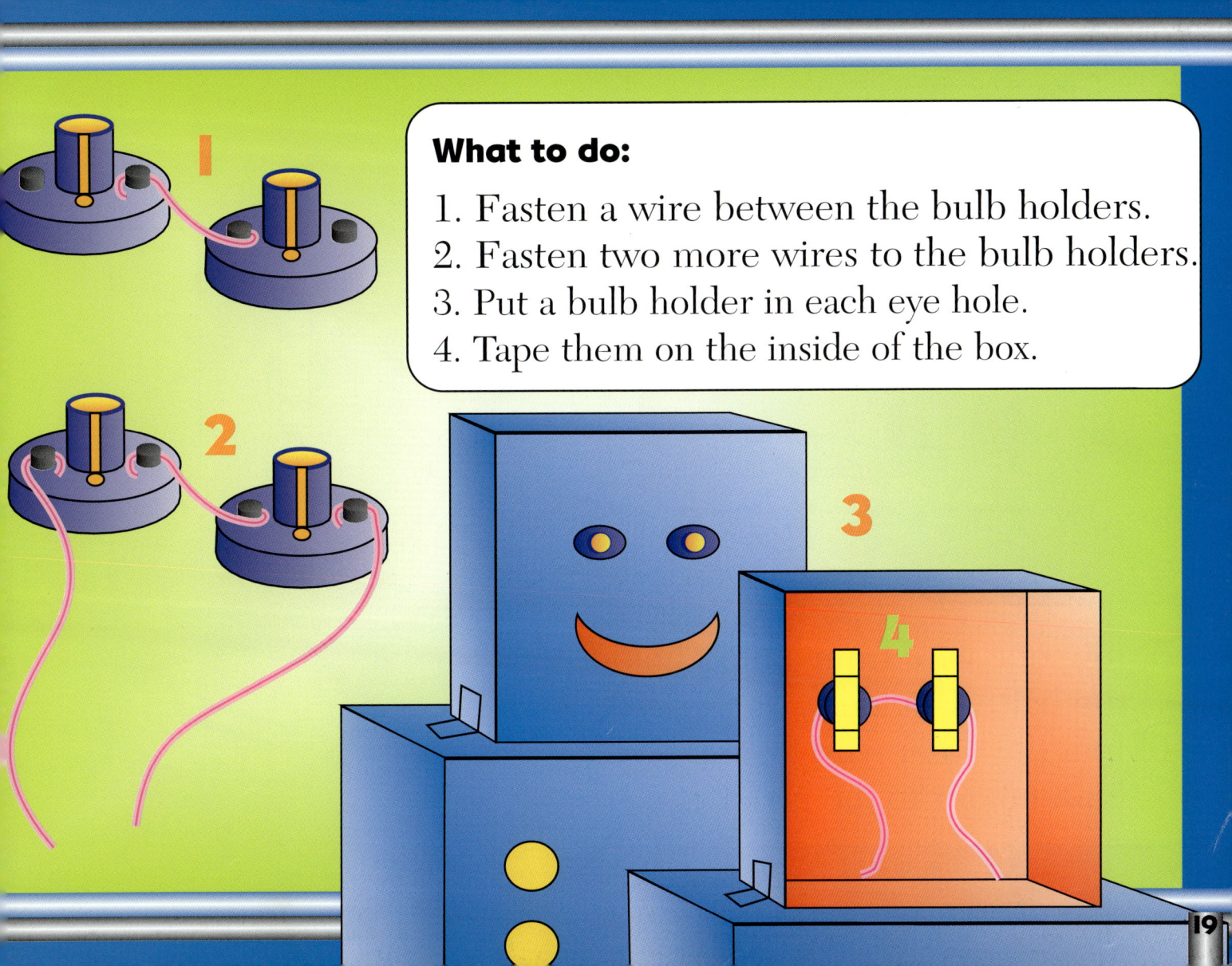

What to do:

1. Fasten a wire between the bulb holders.
2. Fasten two more wires to the bulb holders.
3. Put a bulb holder in each eye hole.
4. Tape them on the inside of the box.

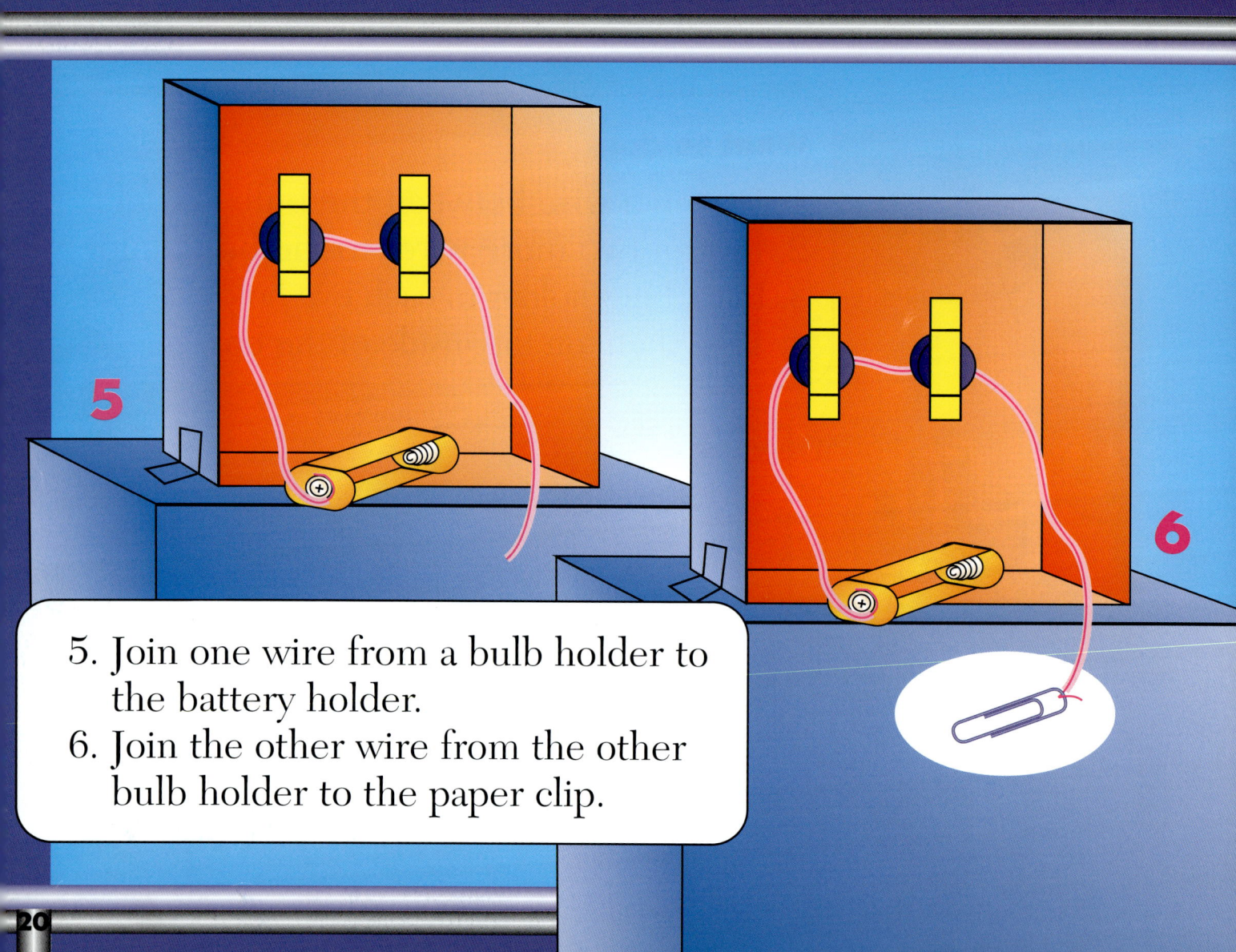

5. Join one wire from a bulb holder to the battery holder.
6. Join the other wire from the other bulb holder to the paper clip.

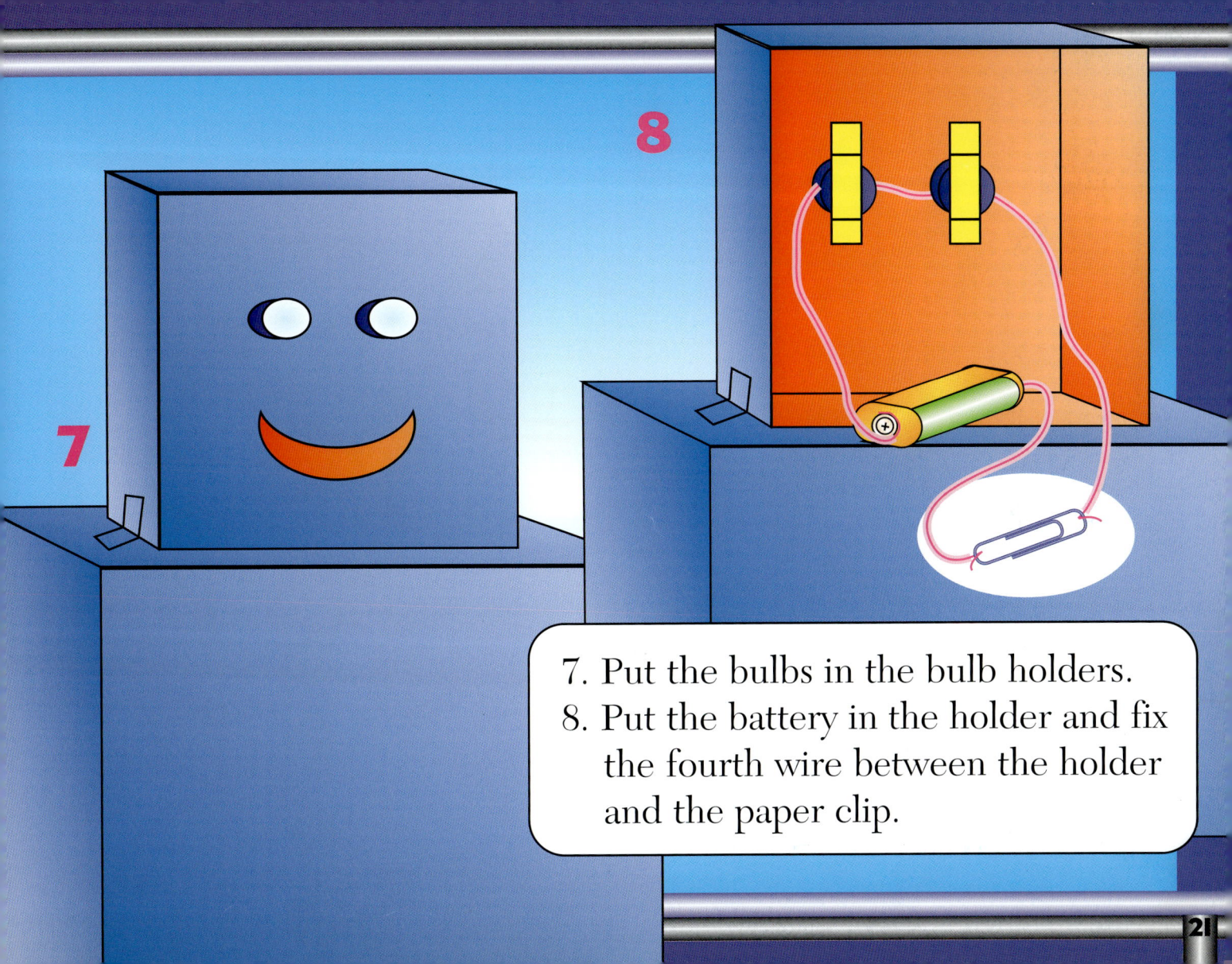

7. Put the bulbs in the bulb holders.
8. Put the battery in the holder and fix the fourth wire between the holder and the paper clip.

The paper clip is the switch. The lights in the eyes of your robot should now be on.

You could use your model as a guard robot. Switch on the lights when it gets dark.

Glossary

automatically – working by itself without humans

intelligent – having a brain

program – set of rules and instructions used to tell a machine how to work

shearing – clipping the fleece off a sheep

Index

be a robot, 11–13
description, 3
jobs, 3, 4–9
    Meldog, 8
    Robosaurus, 9
    Shear Magic, 8
make a robot, 14–22
programming, 10

Bennett Woods School
Library
~~Wardcliff~~ Library Media Center
Okemos, Michigan